ACHIEVING SUCCESS THROUGH DELEGATION

CHOOSING AND PREPARING YOUR DELEGATE

Delegating work motivates your team and frees you up for other tasks, but there is more to delegating than just handing out assignments.

There are many factors and strategies to consider when choosing what to delegate and to whom you should delegate. In this course, you'll explore delegation styles and fundamentals. You'll also learn about preparing and launching a delegation and educating and authorizing delegates.

IDENTIFYING YOUR DELEGATION STYLE

After completing this topic, you should be able to recognize the impact of different delegation styles.

Delegation matters. Delegating ineffectively, communicating insufficiently or vaguely or not following up properly with your delegates and their tasks creates the risk that the work won't be delivered on time or how you expect and need it to be delivered. If your delegates don't deliver, that means your team isn't delivering, and that affects not only you but the whole organization. Just as there are many different types of managers there are different delegation styles. One of the classic styles is the Micromanager.

Micromanagers get that work but they don't give trust or the authority to act. Their supervision is excessive and overbearing. They're constantly watching, asking for updates, and interfering. This creates staff who feel frustrated, constrained, and fearful of criticism. They don't feel trusted and end up becoming overly dependent upon the manager. Micromanaging generates low morale, low self-confidence, and little opportunity for employee personal growth.

Conversely, there is the give and ignore style of delegation. These managers give work and then completely ignore the delegate. They offer little or no instruction, support, supervision, or feedback. You don't know what's expected or required but you are expected to produce anyway. The upshot of the style is overwhelmed employees who can't execute effectively due to a lack of direction.

The work is often poor quality and delivered late. This style of delegation can also result in low morale and a lack of personal growth for employees. And then there are the Scrooges. Scrooges are delegation misers. They don't trust anyone to do anything correctly. Scrooges simply can't allow themselves to delegate. That approach is never going to work well for anyone. Their employees feel powerless, underutilized, and consequently lack motivation. There is no opportunity for growth, development, or learning for their staff.

But before you think that it's all bad news, not all delegation styles are problematic. There is a final category we call delegation stars. These are effective competent delegators. They don't just pass on to their direct reports, they also share information, encouragement, support, and feedback. Their work is given with clear detailed instructions and they follow-up appropriately at the right time.

They provide the responsibility to get the work done and the authority to act. They trust you to do it right and stand ready to provide guidance when needed. The result is productive, efficient, and committed staff who feel part of the organization's success. Staff grow and develop; and the result is a higher level of self-esteem and personal satisfaction. Effective delegation is about achieving the proper balance, the right amount of responsibility, the right authority, the right level of supervision, the right amount of feedback, and the right level of trust.

Think about your own style of delegating. Do you give clear instructions and expectations? Do you follow-up appropriately? Do you supervise providing guidance when needed? Do you give your people the authority to act? If you think about it and are honest with yourself, you'll be able to identify your own style of delegating and adjust it as necessary to achieve delegation stardom.

TO DELEGATE OR NOT TO DELEGATE?

After completing this topic, you should be able to recognize the kinds of tasks that should be delegated.

An important part of developing delegation skills is understanding what types of tasks you should and shouldn't delegate. There are some assignments you should give others to perform but some things you need to handle personally. As a manager what sort of tasks should you keep for yourself? To start with there are personal tasks; things that you can and really should do yourself like getting coffee, picking up your dry cleaning, or scheduling personal appointments.

Not only is it probably quicker and easier to just do these personal tasks tasks yourself they don't contribute anything to your team's development or to the organization as a whole. What would an employee learn or gain from carrying out your personal tasks? And then there are the tasks you have to retain by virtue of your managerial position. And these are things that need managerial authority or responsibility to complete. Having said that don't be too possessive or you'll end up as a delegation Scrooge, someone who can't or won't delegate regardless of circumstance.

Let's consider what these management tasks might entail. They include any tasks that require a level of trust, authority, or responsibility that subordinates or employees don't have. They also include tasks that you by virtue of being the manager simply need to perform. These are core management functions like handling crisis situations or communicating issues and problems to senior management both of which require your knowledge, experience, capability, and authority and feedback tasks such as performance evaluations, coaching team members or issuing warnings for poor performance or inappropriate behavior.

Things like planning, team development are also management tasks that shouldn't be delegated, nor should you delegate any confidential tasks involve sensitive or confidential information. And don't delegate tasks that are unclear or confusing to you. This wastes time, brings no positive impact, and likely requires being revisited and redone anyway. If you don't understand what's expected it's very likely that your people won't either.

While you shouldn't delegate personal or managerial tasks, you absolutely should delegate team tasks. These are tasks that help you develop the team's skills and give you time to lead them. Whenever possible delegate challenging and exciting tasks that your team members want to perform. Tasks that will develop them and get them to the next level and tasks that your team members will be interested in and at best utilize their skills.

Of course you should also delegate repetitive and routine tasks those that have to be carried out on a regular basis and would be time-consuming for you to handle directly. Delegating these tasks will not only develop your team skills and help the organization identify new potential managers and leaders, it also promotes higher productivity and efficiency. It's not enough just to recognize and understand the importance of delegating, you also need to understand what should and what shouldn't be delegated. Some tasks are ideal almost made for sharing. Others you've got to do them yourself.

WHO SHOULD YOU DELEGATE TO?

After completing this topic, you should be able to delegate tasks to the right people.

Different tasks require different skills. Sometimes it can be tricky to match the right people with the right tasks especially when there is a long task list with lots of different skills needed. It's useful to approach delegation in a structured way. First, you need a task list; everything that needs to be delegated. Using this list categorize tasks based on the skills required to complete them.

Add additional factors *[Who's suited to each task?]* like time or quality. Now you've sorted your tasks but you still need to determine who is going to do what. Think about your team members and their individual skill sets. A great way to match your people with tasks is to chart them on a skills matrix. Imagine you're developing a website for a client, the overall task requires different skills: sales and negotiating, creativity and innovation, and technical and analytical skills.

Take those three categories of skills and put them at the ends of a triangle. Put sales, negotiating skills at the top, creative innovative skills one side at the bottom, and technical analytical skills at the other side. Now, think about the people you have available. Let's say you've got a great technical programmer, Toby. He'll do a good job at website development, but he has poor customer skills and he is not particularly creative. Put him in the bottom corner right next to the technical analytical apex.

The more extreme someone's skill set, the closer that person should be to the extreme end. You've also got Kate. Sales and negotiating are her core strengths but she is also pretty creative and often has good design ideas. She'd be on the opposite side from Toby and between sales negotiating and innovative creative. But close her up the line to sales/negotiating because that's her forte.

And finally, you've got Anna, who is similar to Kate but she has got slightly better design skills. So let's position her a little below Kate on the left. Now you can see where everyone fits. Toby will take care of the technical work and implementation but he is going to need some help with the customer, so Kate will lead on that front, and Anna will be tasked with producing creative ideas for the customer. You can use the matrix to show who is best suited to each task and consider availability. Don't assign work to someone who is already overloaded or to someone who won't be around.

And don't forget to take your own schedule and availability into consideration. When you've got a long task list with an array of skills needed and significant work demands to meet, putting the right people onto the right tasks can get complicated. There is no exact science when it comes to matching skills and tasks but a little structure makes things a lot clearer.

PREPARING TO DELEGATE

After completing this topic, you should be able to consider key factors when preparing to delegate a task.

Without proper prior planning delegation can't work. Preparation is key. Effective delegation begins with effective preparation. There is a useful mnemonic device PLEASED that details the components of effective delegation. P is for Prepare; L for Launch and E is Educate; then there is A for Authorize, which means ensuring people have the authority to act; S is for Supervise, which means ensuring they have follow-up; E is for Encourage because you need to motivate people; and the D stands for Development because it's important that your team is developing.

Let's focus on P for Preparation because this is where delegation begins. To ensure you're adequately prepared ask yourself *[Sales/ Negotiating skills.]* six key questions. First ask who? Who should you give the task to? Who is best suited for it? To get the best outcome one person needs to be the lead and everyone needs to be clear on who that is. Then ask what. What needs to be done? What's the specific deliverable?

Don't assume the person assigned to the task automatically knows or understands what you want or expect. Explain it clearly, give examples and ensure that you've provided enough detail and context for your employee to understand what is expected. And be clear about when you need it done, what's the deadline, what's the required delivery date? If you don't establish a clear timeframe you won't get the job done when *[Creative/In-novative skills.]* you need it. Ask where as in where should the active delegating take place.

Should you delegate in private or during a group meeting. Are the details confidential or would it benefit from a group discussion? How might people *[Technical/Analytical skills.]* react to it? The penultimate question to ask is why. People need to clearly understand why they're doing something. Why it matters? Where it fits in the scheme of things? Provide reasons and context. If you're vague or you withhold the information they'll lack either motivation or understanding.

And finally, think about how you want the task done. Is there a special method or approach required; a particular format or process? What form should the output take? A document, presentation or spreadsheet? Don't assume your delegate will know how you want or expect the task to be completed. Now think of your delegates and what they need to be prepared. You can model different types of delegate preparation by thinking of a graph showing scale and motivation levels from low to high where there is low will and low skill.

People won't be motivated or skilled, so their preparation will require more education, encouragement, and direction. Where there is low skill but high will, you'll need to educate and guide your delegate. Where there is high skill but low will, you'll need to encourage and drive them. But if there is high skill and high will, you can trust them to get on with the job. When it comes to delegating effectively, failing to prepare is preparing to fail; to succeed you've got to lay a solid foundation. Use the W questions to drive your preparation and get that P for prepare right.

LAUNCHING DELEGATION WITH THE RIGHT COMMUNICATION

After completing this topic, you should be able to recognize strategies for effective communication of an assignment to a delegate

Delegating tasks isn't always easy or straightforward. You can't just send out a list of deliverables and assume everything will turn out okay. It's essential to first get the basics right. The PLEASED mnemonic is useful for laying out the critical components of an effective delegation process. It begins with P for Prepare, and then there is L for Launch, E for Educate, A for Authorize, S for supervise, E for Encourage, and D for Development.

The second component, the L for Launch is particularly important. When you're launching a delegated task, clear communication is critical to success. Unless you give people the right instruction they won't know what you want. How could they? Think about what needs to be communicated to ensure a successful launch. *[Be clear who lead is.]*

First, be clear about who is taking the lead but also about who else should be involved. Don't delegate a task to a group of people without making clear who is in charge. Either assign a task to one person or assign one person as the lead, otherwise you risk chaos and potential conflict within the team. Next, give clear reasons for the task. Ensure everyone understands why they're doing, what they're doing, and what's expected of them.

If you're vague or secretive, you withhold the information, or you fail to provide the proper context, your delegates won't understand what needs to be done. Be clear about the delivery deadline and the required deliverable. Set a clear start and end date, which should be both realistic and achievable. If you don't tell someone the task needs to be completed it won't be done on time. It's also a mistake to assume the delegate will automatically know what you want.

You have to explain how the results should be delivered and to whom. Successfully delegating a task requires that you also explain how you want it completed, what method or approach is required? Don't assume your delegates will automatically know how you want something done especially if it's a new task or assignment, you don't have to micromanage.

Allow your delegates some freedom to develop their own methods as appropriate, but provide the basics of what you require and stand ready to guide them if and when they get off track. And finally identify checkpoints for providing feedback on progress. Make sure the delegates know when and how to provide you with progress reports or how to ask questions when they have them.

And make sure they understand how the task will be tracked and how feedback will be provided. Launching a task is a critical part of the delegation process and clear, thorough, and detailed communication from the start will ensure that you get it right.

EDUCATING AND AUTHORIZING DELEGATES

After completing this topic, you should be able to recognize how to effectively educate and authorize a delegate.

Successful and effective delegation doesn't just happen; it's a process that requires careful management and it's a process with important individual components. It's useful to refer to the handy mnemonic device PLEASED. This identifies the fundamental components of an effective delegation process. P for Prepare. L for Launch, E for Educate, A for Authorize, S for Supervise, E for Encourage, and D for Development.

When you're giving instructions to a delegate especially for a new task, ensure they know what they're doing then you can guide them through what you want done, the way you want it done. Even an experienced person will need guidance on a new task. From the PLEASED mnemonic consider the second and third stages E for Educate and A for Authorize. Effective delegation requires the delegate to be educated about the task.

First, have a conversation about the task. Don't simply tell them what to do, but invite them into the conversation. You want them to participate and reflect on what's required of them not to feel they're being ordered around. Don't bog them down with excessive details, that comes later; instead be concise, too much detail can overwhelm. Include some pauses in the conversation to give them a chance to ask questions and show they've understood.

Take a moment too to verify that they've understood. Ask questions or get them to summarize what you've discussed. Be sure to explain any terminology or acronyms. Don't assume everyone knows what these words mean. Finally, it's always helpful to give examples to better demonstrate what you're expecting. Try to show them what to do not just tell them, they'll retain the information much better that way.

The next component of effective delegation is to authorize, that is you need to determine the right amount of authority to give your delegate and let them know the depths and limits of their autonomy. Often this is based on their experience. When a delegate is inexperienced it's best to limit decision-making powers and the authority to make decisions on their own. Once they've earned your confidence and trust, you can give more authority.

It's important too to make sure other people involved know about the delegation. Very few tasks can be accomplished alone. When you're getting someone to act on your behalf and making them accountable, ensure that everyone else involved is informed of the situation. A good technique for identifying those involved is what is known as the 360 degree assessment, that means systematically identifying everyone your delegate will have to deal with while carrying out the task.

These are the people that will need to know that your delegate is acting on your behalf and encourages their cooperation. There is an art and a science behind effective delegation. Educating your delegates about the tasks at hand and authorizing them to take the actions necessary to complete them are major components in ensuring successful delegation.

EXERCISE: SKILLFUL DELEGATION

After completing this topic, you should be able to understand how to delegate the right tasks to the right people.

In this exercise, you'll demonstrate how to carefully and thoughtfully manage delegation to ensure its efficacy.

In this exercise, you'll demonstrate that you can:

- recognize different delegation styles,
- recognize the kinds of tasks that should be delegated and who they should be,
- delegated to identify the factors to consider when preparing for and launching delegation, and
- recognize principles for educating and authorizing a delegate.

Question

Match each delegation style to its potential effects. Styles may match to more than one effect.

Options:

A. Micromanager

B. Give and ignore

C. Scrooge

D. Delegation star

Targets:

1. There is low morale and a lack of confidence among employees

2. Employees can't execute instructions

3. Employees feel powerless

4. Employees are productive and efficient

5. Staff members feel like part of organization's success

6. Deliverables are often late

Answer

Because micromanagers withhold trust and authority and tend toward excessive and overbearing supervision, there is often low morale, low self-confidence, and little opportunity for employee personal growth among their teams.

Give and ignore managers offer little or no instruction, support, supervision, or feedback, so employees don't know what's expected or required. These employees can't execute tasks effectively due to a lack of direction.

Because scrooges don't trust anyone to do anything correctly, their employees often feel powerless and underutilized, and consequently lack motivation.

Delegation stars are effective, competent delegators. They share information, encouragement, support, and feedback, which fosters productive, efficient, and committed teams.

Delegation stars provide the responsibility to get the work done and the authority to act, trusting employees to do it right. This results in committed teams who feel like part of the organization's success.

Give and ignore delegators will give work and then completely ignore the delegates, who won't know what's expected or required. As a result, the work is often poor quality and delivered late.

Question

As the account manager for a marketing consultancy firm, you're looking to delegate some of your tasks to your team.

Which tasks should you delegate?

Options:

1. Writing up your notes from this week's team meeting

2. Reading performance reviews of staff members from the smaller firm your company absorbed to see who might be a good addition to your team

3. Coming up with pitch material for a meeting with a large potential client

4. Picking up a wedding anniversary gift

5. Sourcing images and biographies of current and former clients for a publication on the history of the firm

Answer

Option 1: This is a correct option. It is acceptable to delegate repetitive tasks that have to be carried out on a weekly or monthly basis, or at the beginning or end of a project.

Option 2: This is an incorrect option. You should not delegate tasks that are core management functions or that involve confidential, sensitive, or private information.

Option 3: This is a correct option. It's a good idea to delegate tasks that will develop the team's skills and form new leaders.

Option 4: This is an incorrect option. You should carry out personal tasks yourself. They do not help to develop your team

Option 5: This is a correct option. You can delegate tasks that are time consuming or not your concern.

Question

You're manager of a graphic design company that offers web site design, corporate identity, and other services. You're going on vacation.

Match each task to the most suitable individual.

Options:

A. Covering the normal flow of work that arrives

B. Coming up with a strong new poster design at short notice

C. Overseeing a sensitive corporate rebranding for a new client

D. Handling customer communications

Targets:

1. Elliot is a good graphic designer, with experience writing copy and coding. He's good with clients.

2. Rita is an excellent graphic designer with an eye for detail. She's comfortable dealing directly with clients. She's due to be absent for up two months.

3. Lucy is an excellent copywriter with great people skills and some graphics training. Unfortunately, she has no experience up to now shepherding a big project.

4. Harry is an all-rounder who produces solid if unremarkable work. He's good at meeting deadlines, but has no experience leading projects.

Answer

Elliot would be suitable for any of the tasks, but availability and experience make him the best fit for overseeing a sensitive corporate rebranding for a new client.

Rita is best suited to the task of coming up with a strong new poster design at short notice because of the requirements of the task. She could have suited the task of overseeing a corporate rebranding, but her upcoming absence means she won't be around to offer the client continuity and reassurance.

Lucy's skills make her suitable for handling customer communications, but she isn't a good fit for coming up with a strong poster design. She might be able to oversee a sensitive corporate rebranding for a new client, but this important project requires more experience than she has. To develop her skills for this role, she could shadow the person assigned to this task.

Harry's skills make him suitable for covering the normal flow of work that arrives, but he lacks the skills and experience for the other tasks.

Question

You're a pharmaceutical training manager. You're delegating the task of developing and delivering employee training for new machinery.

What should be considered when planning this delegation?

Options:

1. Who has the technical expertise to draft the training materials?

2. Should you explain what needs to be done in a one-to-one setting or in a team meeting?

3. What support and guidance might the delegate need to research and write the training materials?

4. Should you delegate the task to whoever seems most motivated to do it, so long as you approve the work?

5. What will the budget be for this project?

Answer

Option 1: *This option is correct. When delegating a task, you need to make sure that one person is clearly assigned and that this person has the right skills to complete the task satisfactorily.*

Option 2: *This option is correct. This is a type of "where" question. The setting for telling the delegate about the new task depends on whether the communication is personal or technical in nature. In this case, as the task is technical, a team environment might be better.*

Option 3: *This option is correct. This is an example of a "how" question, and is aimed at finding out what special instructions the delegate will need in order to accomplish the task.*

Option 4: *This option is incorrect. When choosing a particular person for a task, you need to be clear in your own mind why this person is the* *right choice, and not just because they "seem" motivated.*

Option 5: This option is incorrect. The budget isn't something that affects how you delegate a task. Instead, you need to focus on issues such as who should complete the task, why that particular person, and what the deliverables are.

Question

A hotel manager is delegating the task of organizing and managing an important upcoming private function.

What should be communicated?

Options:

1. The identity of who's taking the lead in organizing and managing the event

2. The standards required in terms of organization, presentation, and service

3. Relevant deadlines for finalizing menus and the list of attendees

4. Basic guidelines on what's required and how the event should be organized

5. The specific measurable that will be monitored and when progress reports are required

6. Detailed accounts of previous functions that were not organized properly

7. Information on expected guests' menu preferences

Answer

Option 1: This option is correct. It's important to be clear about who's taking the lead and who's in charge. Otherwise, there's a risk of confusion and conflict within the team.

Option 2: This option is correct. Everyone needs to understand what's expected of them and know exactly what needs to be done.

Option 3: This option is correct. Setting clear and achievable deadlines is an important aspect of communicating with the delegate. If the delegate doesn't know when something needs to be done, it might not be done on time.

Option 4: *This option is correct. When delegating, you should explain how you want the task completed, including general guidelines on the method or approach that should be used.*

Option 5: *This option is correct. Delegates should know how and when to provide progress reports and understand how the task will be tracked.*

Option 6: *This option is incorrect. Although this information could be useful to the delegate, it's not necessary for the smooth functioning of the delegation process.*

Option 7: *This option is incorrect. This information would be helpful in planning the menu for the function, but it's not part of the delegation process.*

Question

Effective delegation entails educating the delegate about the task and giving the delegate authority to act.

What are some examples of effective education and authorization?

Options:

1. The manager invites the delegate to discuss the task and reflect on what's required

2. The manager only goes into detail where strictly necessary, ensuring the delegate isn't overwhelmed

3. The manager saves time by assuming the delegate understands commonly used acronyms

4. The manager talks the delegate through examples in order to better explain what's needed

5. The manager considers the level of authority the delegate needs to perform the task

6. The manager ensures that all others likely to be involved are briefed about the delegation

Answer

Option 1: *This option is correct. Instead of simply telling a delegate what to do, it's better to have a conversation about the task. The aim is for the delegate to participate and reflect on what's required.*

Option 2: *This option is correct. It's a mistake to overwhelm the delegate with excessive detail. Only go into real detail where and when necessary.*

Option 3: *This option is incorrect. It's necessary to explain any terminology or acronyms, rather than assuming everyone knows what these words mean.*

Option 4: *This option is incorrect. It's better to illustrate what's needed through examples, effectively showing rather than telling.*

Option 5: *This option is correct. An important step is for the delegator to determine the right amount of authority to give the delegate, and then let the delegate know the depths and limits of their autonomy.*

Option 6: *This option is correct. It's essential to tell everyone who your delegate will have to deal with while carrying out the task about the delegation, ensuring the delegate receives all necessary cooperation and assistance.*

GETTING WHAT YOU EXPECT FROM YOUR DELEGATE

The delegation process doesn't end with a decision to delegate. In many respects, that's just the beginning. Getting good delegation results depends on the right level of supervision, including follow-up, encouragement and handling mistakes.

In this course, you'll learn how to supervise and motivate your delegates. You'll also learn how to identify and avoid engaging in negative or demotivating behaviors. In addition, you'll learn how to respond when things go wrong and provide constructive criticism.

1. Supervision: How Much?
2. Encouraging and Motivating a Delegate
3. How Not to Motivate a Delegate
4. Delegation: When Things Go Wrong
5. How to Deliver Constructive Criticism
6. Exercise: Supervising and Encouraging Your Delegate

SUPERVISION: HOW MUCH?

After completing this topic, you should be able to recognize appropriate actions to take to follow up on a delegated task.

When it comes to delegating, you need to control the process taking ownership and managing it. And that means paying attention to the individual components of effective delegation. You might know of the pneumatic device, PLEASED, that details these components. P stands for Prepare, L for Launch and E for Educate. A stands for Authorize giving people the authority to act and S stands for Supervise. E is for Encourage, which is about motivating people and D stands for Development.

Let's now focus on S for Supervise. The right level of supervision falls somewhere between the extremes of micromanagement on the one hand and the give and ignore approach on the other. It's not helpful to delegate a task and then constantly meddle and request a constant stream of status updates. Nor is it helpful to delegate something and then walk away entirely, leaving your delegates to their own devices.

You need to find the right balance. The first thing to do to ensure the effective supervision or a follow-up of a delegate is to set reasonable checkpoints. Setting checkpoints at the right intervals means you won't have to micromanage. You'll get the assurance that your delegates are on track and they're completing the task in the way you expect.

You can use the checkpoints to ask questions, review progress and provide more direction as warranted. It's also important to make yourself available for guidance and make sure the delegates know you're available. And let them know they can approach you when needed and what they can expect from you. Set aside time for guiding and providing help in any way that may be necessary. And then trust your delegates to deliver.

It's important that delegates see and genuinely believe that you trust them to execute. Let them get on with the task you've assigned. It's okay, necessary in fact to ask to be informed of progress. But don't be overly controlling. The final aspects of effective supervision are coaching the delegates through difficulties and then recognizing their successes. When difficulties arise, work with them to address the issues. Coach, advise and show them how to take things forward. But don't actually do the work yourself.

They need to learn self-sufficiency in order to develop themselves. And this may mean pointing them to other people who may be able to help or other resources they can use to get back on track. By the same token, make sure you recognize even their smallest successes. This keeps them motivated, enthusiastic and ensures that you'll get the results you need. Supervision of delegates is a key component of effective delegation.

It's important to get the balance right between being to hands-on and too distant. Setting checkpoints, ensuring you're available for guidance, trusting your delegates, coaching them through problems in difficult times and recognizing their successes help achieve that balance.

ENCOURAGING
AND MOTIVATING
A DELEGATE

After completing this topic, you should be able to recall actions that motivate a delegate.

Effective delegation doesn't just happen on its own, it requires your active management and engagement. An active management means not only paying attention to the details, but also keeping your delegates motivated. Consider the pneumonic device, PLEASED, that takes us through the individual components of effective delegation. Again, P stands for Prepare, L for Launch, E for Educate, A for Authorize, S for Supervise, E for Encourage and D stands for Development. For now, let's focus on E, Encourage.

Motivating your delegates and keeping them engaged and encouraged is critical to successful delegation. To motivate a delegate, be positive, solution oriented and set a good example. It's important to remember that a delegate's motivation starts with your own behavior. You are their role model. You need to set a good example through your leadership. You need to be positive and upbeat about the tasks and processes you're asking them to take on.

If you treat the work as drudgery or something you simply want to get rid of, they will too. Along those lines make sure your delegate understands the context of what they're doing, how the task at hand fits into the bigger picture. When people understand the context, they'll understand the importance of the task, why it matters and by into the process. Also let them know what's in it for them. After all, they're likely developing new skills or stepping up to a new challenge.

If the work is repetitive or potentially boring, putting it in the context of the results for the team or the company helps keep you delegate motivated with the end game in the bottom line. But even when tasks are tedious, they're still some ways you can keep things interesting. Sometimes it's necessary to shake things up, give different people different tasks. Once a task is mastered or performed for an extended period, reassign it and let your delegate try something new.

Give them a chance to empower themselves. Perhaps giving them a leeway to improve the process, supervise the work of another employee or add a little extra challenge to the task. If possible jump in yourself from time to time. It can help earn their respect and show you're not above getting your own hands dirty. It's also a chance to find out what's really going on in the trenches.

Successful delegation depends on keeping your delegates enthused and motivated. The tasks you're delegating won't always be fresh or exciting. Some will be mundane tasks that just need to get done. Being positive, setting a good example, explaining the context and occasionally shaking things up help keep your delegate's fires burning. And when your team is engaged and motivated the results will reflect it.

HOW NOT TO MOTIVATE A DELEGATE

After completing this topic, you should be able to identify demotivating actions that should be avoided.

This sort of work you may need to delegate won't always thrill your delegates. More often they'll be mundane, everyday chores that just need to get done. Even so you need your team to be motivated and on track. Good results come from motivation and enthusiasm. While there are plenty of good ways to go about providing motivation, there are also some disastrous ones that you have to learn to avoid.

Managers want the best for their team and their organization and motivated high-performing delegates deliver on behalf of their managers. But managers sometimes get it wrong. Acting in ways or using methods that are counterproductive, killing motivation instead of building it. There are a number of common mistakes and negative behaviors to avoid. The first behavior is you must absolutely avoid are threatening or publicly criticizing a delegate.

Threaten someone and they'll focus on the threat not what needs to change. It's counterproductive and it's not professional. And criticizing someone in public will only cause them to feel ashamed in front of their colleagues and that reduces morale. Both behaviors breed resentment and animosity and they kill motivation. Angry *[Indiscernible]* delegates don't deliver.

It's worth pointing out too that managers who make a habit of threatening or publicly criticizing subordinates eventually erode their own credibility and authority. Another mistake is failing to praise your delegate's successes. Everyone response to praise. Good work, effort and successful results should be recognized and celebrated. If successes and positive results are ignored, people start wondering whether there is any point trying or working hard next time around.

[Failing to follow up] Failure to follow up is another big mistake. If you don't follow up, you won't know if progress is being made or when your delegate is having problems. And you won't know whether they're staying motivated. Following up shows you're interested that you care and that you recognize the value of the task. Don't set unachievable goals and unrealistic deadlines.

Assigning tasks or setting goals that simply aren't achievable is a sure-fire way to destroy motivation. Ensuring the goals and deadlines you set are reasonable and achievable will ensure that your team believes you understand what they're facing. Being secretive is yet another common error to avoid. Tell your people what you're delegating and why you're delegating it to them. Provide context and they'll understand the what, why, when and how things need to be done.

Finally, avoid being closed off to your delegate's suggestions or ideas. Show regard for your team's abilities and positive input. Overtime, they'll discover better ways to accomplish the tasks you've assigned them. It's important to listen to them and then give them the freedom to get on with the task. Ultimately, when you're trying to motivate others threats, warnings or negative behavior don't work; instead be positive, encouraging and available, setting a good example and recognizing successes that's where motivation comes from.

DELEGATION: WHEN THINGS GO WRONG

After completing this topic, you should be able to respond appropriately to bad results from delegation.

In business as in all walks of life things sometimes go awry when delegating. It's tempting to lose your cool and start blaming people when things go wrong without really understanding what happened. Knee jerk reactions never help. Perhaps the team badly underperformed, but could one of the root causes be that your delegation failed in some way. Don't lay blame without first understanding the *[How to respond.]* root causes of the issue.

First, take a step back and try to understand the nature of the problem or mistake. Pause for a moment to determine what exactly went wrong. Was the delivery late? Was there a budget overrun? Was it a quality issue? Sometimes the job gets done, but gets done poorly. Work backward from the problem until you know exactly why the result was unsatisfactory. Next, review your delegation process. Did you delegate properly?

Examine the PLEASED mnemonic. Did you follow the fundamental components of effective delegation prepare, launch, educate, authorize, supervise, encourage and develop? If things have gone wrong, go back and think about your contribution before blaming anyone else.

These done, you can now investigate and identify the root cause of the problem. Perhaps your delegation process was to blame, but maybe that wasn't the cause or not the only cause where they're unforeseen events and if so should or could these have been anticipated. Did you take on too much risk or underestimate the scope of the effort and the required resources?

Delegate too much authority perhaps your delegate failed for some personal reason outside of work. Any number of factors could be at play. Having identified the root cause of the problem it's time to get feedback from the delegate. Get their opinion on what went right and what went wrong. Do they understand the root cause of the problem and its ultimate impact? Review the relevant issues and what could be done better next time.

Decide whether some specific training is needed. Consider what might motivate them to seek help or identify problems earlier in the process next time. Once you've worked out what went wrong, agree on a joint action plan for improvement. What needs to change, what must be done better and how will the team adjust.

Good managers take the time and effort to involve their team in identifying lessons learned. And focusing on moving forward in a positive direction they take time for a one-to-one sessions with their delegates. Debriefing them, listening to their views and adjusting their own actions accordingly. When things go wrong, its human nature to react without taking the time to think things through.

We've all been guilty of it, but lashing out and placing blame is not an effective response. It's always better to respond calmly and methodically determining what went wrong, why it went wrong and how it can be fixed for the future.

HOW TO DELIVER CONSTRUCTIVE CRITICISM

After completing this topic, you should be able to deliver constructive criticism to improve performance.

No one likes criticism, but it's a part of working life. When you've got to give criticism, it's most productive to do it in a positive way. Think of delivering criticism like making a sandwich. The first layer, the bread, should be a positive compliment, something the person has done well. The filling is the criticism, the meat, cheese, lettuce, and condiments of your message. And finally, the top layer of bread is an action plan with follow up ending things on a positive and productive note.

Let's pull those ingredients apart again and consider how they fit properly together. Delivering constructive criticism should begin with a positive compliment. People react positively when complimented about something done well. They're less defensive and more open to ideas and ways to change. It allows them to take the criticism that follows as a specific instance and not a general condemnation. Start by praising what went well before turning to the not so well.

You're critiquing, not attacking. Keep your delivery, tone of voice and body language positive. After the positive compliment comes the criticism or what needs to change. Don't jump straight into the criticism. First, ask for your delegate's thoughts and opinions. Ask your delegate if there is anything they might have done differently and get their opinion on how things went. You'll be surprised how often they'll know what's gone wrong and readily acknowledge it when they feel safe and not under fire.

They may even have their own ideas about how to improve. And that makes it much easier to work with them to get better results. If they don't know or acknowledge what went wrong, you'll have to tell them. Focus on their behavior on the process and how they went about it. This isn't about their false as a person, it's about an action or behavior what the person did not who the person is. Ensure your delivery is concise and to the point.

Once they understand the problem move on, don't [deliver] [Phonetic] the issue. Agreeing on an action plan and follow up is the final part of the criticism sandwich. This is how you leave things on a positive note. Here is where you both agree on how they're going to improve and move forward. Agree on clear learning points and what steps you're each responsible for in order to ensure that improvement happens.

Make them feel that they've got every chance to succeed and show them that you mean it. Most importantly, remember to plan for follow up. Schedule times when you can offer help and guidance, but also for checking in on their progress. Giving criticism requires thought and care. Don't do it when you are angry.

Don't make it personal. Both are counterproductive; instead stay calm and positive. Focus on the process and the behavior not the individual. Remember, you're making a sandwich with positive comments and action plans on the outside and constructive useful criticism on the inside. The tasty results are moving forward with better performance and better results for you, your team and the organization.

EXERCISE: SUPERVISING AND ENCOURAGING YOUR DELEGATE

After completing this topic, you should be able to use appropriate supervision and feedback techniques to enhance a delegate's performance.

In this exercise, you'll demonstrate your understanding of appropriate delegation supervision techniques, including how to follow up with, encourage, motivate, and, when necessary, constructively criticize your delegate.

In this exercise, you'll demonstrate that you can:

- recognize strategies for supervising and effectively motivating your delegates,
- respond appropriately when a delegated task doesn't work out well, and
- deliver constructive criticism to a delegate.

Question

As a call center supervisor, you ask John to job shadow a more senior employee, Dave, to get experience in customer retention calls.

What are appropriate actions to follow up on the delegated task?

Options:

1. Ask John to speak to you if he has any problems, but tell him you trust that he can organize the time with Dave on his own

2. Arrange to meet with John on the following Friday to check on his progress

3. Ask John to tell you what he thinks are the key things he still needs to learn

4. When you notice John seems confused on calls, privately ask Dave to report back to you any problems he notices

5. Tell John you'll be busy for a while so he should ask Dave if he has any questions

Answer

Option 1: *This option is correct. Make yourself available to the delegate if he runs into problems, but demonstrate that you trust him by letting him organize the task on his own.*

Option 2: *This option is correct. When you delegate work, identify the dates on which you want to receive feedback about progress.*

Option 3: *This option is correct. Involve the delegate in setting expectations for the delegated task. The more you involve him in negotiating and agreeing to the terms, the more he'll feel responsible for delivering on the task.*

Option 4: *This option is incorrect. If you notice a delegate is struggling, give advice and coaching or point him to the resources he needs. Don't ask someone else to do that for you.*

Option 5: *This option is incorrect. When you delegate a task, make sure the delegate knows you're available for guidance, and be sure to make yourself available.*

Question

A training manager who develops webinars to deliver training wants her assistant, Joe, to help build webinar content.

Which of her statements would encourage and motivate Joe?

Options:

1. "With everything else going on with the company expansion, I just don't have time to give them the attention they need. I'd like you to help develop the content."

2. "One webinar a week for the next eight weeks is my goal. I know you can do this."

3. "I've been meaning to ask you about tool kits – what are your thoughts on hosting everything on a file sharing site?"

4. "I really need you to run with this. I won't be available much for a few days, so if

5. you have any questions, you should ask one of the other team members." 5. "You know how I've been working the webinars?

Answer

Option 1: *This option is correct. In explaining why this task is important and putting it in the context of what's happening in the organization as a whole, the manager motivates Joe and helps him see the importance of the task.*

Option 2: *This option is correct. The manager is motivating Joe by being positive and encouraging him.*

Option 3: *This option is correct. By asking about another project Joe is working on, the manager is showing an interest in his work. That's an example of motivating behavior.*

Option 4: *This option is incorrect. To motivate a delegate, you need to be available to them, to answer any questions they have about the task. The manager won't be available to answer Joe's initial questions, which could be demotivating.*

Option 5: *This option is incorrect. To motivate Joe, the manager* *should provide more details about the context of the webinars. This question doesn't give Joe much context.*

Question

As the senior copywriter at an ad agency, you've asked a junior copywriter, Bill, to come up with some fresh ideas for a client's new campaign.

Identify examples of demotivating behavior to avoid.

Options:

1. Get Bill to try harder by explaining you'll assign the task to someone else unless his efforts improve

2. Enthusiastically tell Bill how much you like his initial ideas, and tell him to keep up the good work

3. Avoid checking in with Bill so he doesn't feel like you don't fully trust him

4. Ensure deadlines are easily achievable and realistic, allowing some leeway for Bill's inexperience

5. Don't tell Bill who or what the campaign is for, in order to ensure his ideas are completely fresh and novel

6. Regularly ask Bill for his opinions or ideas on the overall campaign and his views on how the agency handles it

Answer

Option 1: This option is correct. It's a mistake to threaten a delegate as it makes them focus on the threat, not what needs to change. It's counterproductive and dramatically reduces motivation.

Option 2: This option is incorrect. Good work, effort, and successful results should be praised. People's motivation increases when they're praised.

Option 3: This option is correct. It's a mistake not to follow up with a delegate. Following up shows the delegate that you're interested.

Option 4: This option is incorrect. It's essential that goals and dead-

lines are reasonable and achievable. Otherwise, the delegate will quickly become demotivated and disillusioned.

Option 5: *This option is correct. Being secretive and withholding information from a delegate will inevitably have a negative impact on the delegate's motivation.*

Option 6: *This option is incorrect. Being open to your delegate's suggestions or ideas is a good idea. Otherwise, they'll feel you don't have trust or regard for their abilities, which will result in demotivation.*

Question

As sales director at an auto dealership, you know one of your sales team, Emma, is struggling with a task you gave her, converting telephone enquiries.

Which responses are appropriate?

Options:

1. Ask Emma's supervisor if the problem is Emma's manner or her lack of product knowledge

2. Think about whether you provided Emma with all the information and training she needed to succeed

3. Determine what has ultimately caused Emma's poor performance

4. Tell Emma the buck stops with her and that her poor performance is frustrating the customers

5. Create a detailed cheat sheet for Emma to keep at her station, outlining the actions she can take for each specific call scenario

Answer

Option 1: *This option is correct. To respond, first try to understand the nature of the poor results. Is it time, budget, or quality?*

Option 2: *This option is correct. When delegation goes wrong, review your approach. Perhaps you missed a key step in the PLEASED approach, such as recognizing a training need.*

Option 3: *This option is correct. If you get poor results from delegation, investigate and identify the root cause. Was the problem caused by the delegation process?*

Option 4: *This option is incorrect. Actually, the buck still stops with you when you delegate work. Simply blaming Emma will not help the situation. You need to work with her to find out what's gone wrong and how it can be fixed.*

Option 5: *This option is incorrect. If you get poor results from a delegation, it's better to collaborate with the delegate on a joint improvement action plan, rather than imposing a plan you've created on your own.*

Question

Your delegate Zach is performing badly due to poor technical knowledge.

Give him constructive criticism by matching each feedback stage to the appropriate comment. Not all comments will have a match.

Options:

A. Start the feedback with...

B. Next, say...

C. End the feedback with...

Targets:

1. "I'm impressed with how much you've learned so far."

2. "I've noticed that you're not clear on certain technical details. What do you think you can do to improve?"

3. "Let's get together tomorrow to plan a joint approach to this so we can keep the momentum going. I really appreciate the effort you're putting in on this."

4. "I can't think of anything good to say right now. I know you're trying, but we have a lot of work to do to resolve

this."

5. "I think you're just not tough enough for this job. You need to be more confident and assertive."

Answer

This is how you should start the feedback, the first layer of the feedback sandwich. Delivering a compliment, no matter how small, shows that you've noticed something good about what the delegate has done so far.

This is the middle layer in the feedback sandwich. This is where you give the criticism. Focus on the behavior and process, not on the person. Avoid the blame game, and involve them in devising a solution.

This is the last layer in the sandwich, how you should end the feedback. In this layer, you get positive again. You finish on a positive note and clearly agree on actions and next steps.

This isn't an example of a part of the feedback sandwich. When delivering criticism, it's important to find one positive thing to say, even if it's a small thing.

This isn't an example of a part of the feedback sandwich. When you're delivering criticism, it's important to focus on behavior and process, not on the person and their personality traits.

TAKING YOUR TEAM TO THE NEXT LEVEL WITH DELEGATION

There are many components of effective delegation. Getting the job done is the obvious first objective, but it's not the only or even always the primary objective. Staff development is a crucial aspect of delegation.

It takes you and your team to the next level. In this course, you'll learn how to develop your team mitigating common delegation risks. You'll also learn how to assess and develop your delegation technique.

SORIN DUMITRASCU

1. Development through Delegation
2. Manage Delegation to Develop Your Team
3. Avoiding Common Delegation Risks
4. Reflecting on Your Delegation Technique
5. Developing Your Delegation Technique
6. Exercise: Develop Your Team by Delegating

DEVELOPMENT THROUGH DELEGATION

After completing this topic, you should be able to delegate a task to a person in a way that develops them.

One of your responsibilities as a manager is to elevate your team professionally, to raise their skill and performance levels to develop them. *[Developing your team.]* Delegation helps you do this using varying levels of trust, authority and responsibility as you assign new tasks. First, consider the mnemonic device, P.L.E.A.S.E.D, which details the components of effective delegation. P stands for Prepare, L for Launch, E for Educate, A for Authorize, S for Supervise, E for Encourage and D stands for Development.

For now, we'll concern ourselves with D for Development. You can use increasing levels of trust, authority and responsibility to develop your team as you're delegating. Now, consider the trust pyramid. It's a pyramid with six levels, beginning with Tell at the bottom and building up through Ask, Recommend, Approve, Act and at the top Inform. Each level represents an increased level of autonomy and responsibility.

As your team members move up through the levels, you're giving them more freedom and developing them as both a person and employee. Keep this in mind as you're delegating. Let's examine each level separately. The bottom level is Tell. When you're delegating to an inexperienced team member or for the first time you need to tell them exactly what to do step by step. When they complete one task or part of a process, you tell them what to do next.

At the next level, encourage the more experienced delegate to ask about or investigate the task. Let them explore how to complete what needs to be done then advice them on how to proceed. Moving up another trust level, ask the delegate to recommend how to proceed and then make the decision together based on their recommendation. As your people develop further, they'll reach a point where you just need to approve and sign off on their decisions.

You're showing trust and the judgment they've developed as they climb the pyramid. At the second-highest level, you're giving them added authority to act based on their own judegment. Within established boundaries, you're allowing the delegate the autonomy to work through the task with minimal oversight and restriction. Eventually, they reach the informed level.

Here you're granting them responsibility and authority to go ahead with tasks as they see fit only requiring them to keep you informed. Development their delegation is a balancing act. As a manager, you use trust, authority and responsibility and increasing levels to develop your team. Junior staff don't have the experience or knowledge to work on their own.

Experienced staff don't want to be led by the hand or mired in tasks that don't take advantage of their skills and abilities. Using increasing levels of trust, responsibility and authority, you can develop your team individually strengthening their performance as you go along. And if they're performing better everyone benefits individual and team alike.

MANAGE DELEGATION TO DEVELOP YOUR TEAM

After completing this topic, you should be able to delegate in a way that develops an employee.

Delegating is not just about offloading tasks to reduce your own workload, there is much more to it, including the opportunity to develop your employees it's not automatic. It doesn't just happen on its own and not every way of delegating is effective at developing employees. There are three core principles that will help you delegate in a way that fosters development. First, whenever possible, make it a challenge, stretch the delegate.

When you've got a task to assign, take the time to consider who on your team may benefit the most from completing it. What may be a routine monotonous chore for one employee something they've done a 100 times before may well be a new and exciting opportunity for another. Will it take them out of their comfort zone and genuinely challenge them that employee will likely be motivated and excited about it and completing it will contribute to their development.

And the more experienced person will be grateful to be given a different challenge too. Second, enable and coach your delegates to develop new skills. Imagine you've got a recurring task that require some particular knowledge or skill, and further it needs to be done on a regular schedule. Why give it to the same person every time? It makes more sense to identify someone else on the team who'd benefit from and has shown an interest in learning that new skill as well as helping the team member develop this benefits the organization increasing the number of skilled workers.

Third, incrementally increase the level of trust you extend to your people as they earn it. Sometimes managers need to take a little bit of a risk taking calculated chances with their people. That means little by little showing them more trust each time they prove themselves. For example, suppose you've got a particular employee you want to develop, look for opportunities that will help them learn and build upon new skills and knowledge. Is there a task you can assign that will guide that employee through increased levels of responsibility and encourage more autonomy?

The idea is not to suddenly give someone absolute trust and unlimited freedom but rather allowing them to earn increasing levels of trust bit by bit as they prove themselves capable. If done properly, delegating can be a powerful tool for developing employees. It's about challenging them to rise to the next level coaching them and giving them opportunities to learn new skills.

And as they do extending more trust guiding them to new levels of responsibility and authority. This leads to a more motivated, more skilled and more capable team better developed to produce superior results.

AVOIDING COMMON DELEGATION RISKS

After completing this topic, you should be able to recognize tactics for avoiding delegation risks.

The benefits of delegation are widely understood. Necessary tasks are completed, organizational outcomes improve and employees are developed. It's a win-win all around. But whether you consider delegating well in art or science, the techniques of how to do it effectively must be mastered. It's important that you get it right, but it's essential that you don't get it wrong for yourself and your team. You must learn to recognize, mitigate and avoid the most common delegation risks and mistakes.

[Avoid overextending.] Perhaps, the greatest delegation risk is overextending your people. When you're delegating a task that carries a high-level of authority and autonomy you need to be careful asking for too much too soon without the appropriate support has a real downside. Consider this, when you assign a task, granting your delegate just the right level of authority and autonomy there is a balance or symmetry between the task and the delegate.

Chances are it'll go well and when things go well the delegate gains the confidence to take on and achieve more next time. But if you delegate too much responsibility to an unprepared or inexperienced employee the opposite happens. At best, it's a recipe for an overwhelmed, frustrated and demoralized employee.

At worst, your delegate loses confidence and may even disengage resulting in the double negative of an unmotivated employee completing a task poorly. So, keep that in mind when you're delegating. When granting authority and autonomy, think about the development level of you delegate. Make sure you're not overextending your people and giving them bigger bites than they're able to chew. Do allow [phonetic] responsibility carefully.

[Avoid demotivating.] Conversely, the second major delegation risk is demotivating people at the opposite extreme. Don't delegate tasks to experienced people that will bore them that kills motivation in a heartbeat. This is an especially prevalent consideration for your people already operating at the top-level who already have earned your total trust.

For instance, take someone who is accustomed to being given high-level tasks that carry a lot of responsibility and autonomy. What's going to happen if you suddenly assign a low-level task that they consider menial? Most likely, the result will be boredom, frustration, and demotivation. Instead when delegating, give these people a chance to have diverse opportunities to work on new tasks, learn new skills and take on new challenges.

That's how you develop, excite and motivate your team. The end result is a net positive for you, for them and the entire organization. Knowing these risks and being able to identify the potential pitfalls is a big part of achieving your delegate balance. On the one hand, don't force people to be overextended. On the other hand, don't negatively impact their motivation. Assigning tasks appropriately is important for properly practicing the art and science of good delegation.

REFLECTING ON YOUR DELEGATION TECHNIQUE

After completing this topic, you should be able to review your delegation performance in a structured way.

If you're like most of the working population you routinely find yourself rushing from one task to the next. Frantically, trying to keep up with your workload and get the next job done that doesn't leave much time or bandwidth to pause. Look back and reflect on what you're doing or how you're doing it. But if you don't make the time to think about your performance, you're never going to improve. That's what you tell your people. Now listen to your own advice. It's important to reflect on how well you're doing your job and that includes your delegation technique.

Gauging the success of your delegation performance requires a structured examination and you can use the mnemonic, P.L.E.A.S.E.D, to create a structured checklist to help you. The P.L.E.A.S.E.D mnemonic is a framework for thinking about delegation. It begins with P for Prepare. Ask yourself, did I take time to think about the tasks I was assigning and who I assigned it to? Did you assign the right tasks to the right people? Did you properly prepare them for it? L is for Launch.

Did you launch your delegate into the assignment properly and clearly? Were you clear about what you wanted done and who you wanted to do it? Clear about when and how you wanted it done? E is for Educate. Did you give thought to matching your delegate skills to their assigned tasks? Did you help the team to get started? Did you provide instruction, support and guidance?

Now consider the A of PLEASED, which stands for Authorize. Did you give your delegates the right level of authority and did you tell everyone who needed to know that the delegate was acting on your behalf and with your authority? And did you truly trust the delegate giving them the freedom to act on that authority without fear of being chastised? S is for Supervise. Did you set regular checkpoints and follow up? Did you provide enough supervision too much? Do you think the team felt adequately supported? The E stands for Encourage.

Did you coach and encourage delegates? Were they enthused and motivated? Were you helpful offering suggestions and assistance? Finally, D is for Develop. Did you sit down with the delegate at the end of the task to review how things went and what could be improved next time? Do you genuinely believe that you challenge the delegate and help them improve their skills and knowledge base?

These are the goals of delegation. Taking a moment to reflect on your performance is the most direct way to figure out what you are doing well and where you can perform better. Ask yourself tough questions and be honest with your answers. Improvement only comes with proactive reflection.

DEVELOPING YOUR DELEGATION TECHNIQUE

After completing this topic, you should be able to get feedback from others to help develop your delegation technique.

Most of us are poor judges of our own work. It's hard to be objective about your performance when you're personally and emotionally connected to it. It's certainly useful, even imperative to reflect on on your delegation technique and performance. But any effort to understand your own strengths and weaknesses requires getting feedback from others.

This means talking to your team and collecting their input about your delegation style and performance. After all, they're the ones on the receiving end, experiencing it up close and personal. Fortunately, there are methods for getting feedback from others in a way that will help you develop your delegation technique.

First, simply talk to your team. Once you've reflected on and assessed your own performance, go and talk with them directly and this is critical. Make it clear that you want them to speak openly and candidly that you don't want them holding back or sugarcoating anything they have to say. If necessary, give them the chance to give their feedback privately in confidence or even anonymously.

Second, make it clear that you want to improve. Ensure that your team members understand and really believe that you're serious about wanting to improve your delegation style and make sure that they understand the importance of their feedback in this. Third, listen and ask leading questions. Assure them that you value, respect and genuinely want to hear their views and give them the time and space to express those views.

If the conversation is drifting or losing focus, don't be afraid to ask some direct leading questions to get the honest information you need. For instance, ask, do you feel you were adequately supported in the task or do you think the level of supervision was too much or overbearing? Then don't interrupt, make it clear you're listening and be open to their responses. Once you've talked to your team, collate their feedback.

Collect everything but focus especially on feedback that pertains to your delegation style. Did you hit the right notes when it came to the individual components of effective delegation? How did you do with preparation and launch? Did you educate your team fully and to the extent they required? Did you properly assign authorization and responsibilities? Did you supervise and get feedback as the task proceeded?

Were you successful in your efforts to encourage and motivate the team? And were you able to develop your delegates? Nobody is born in delegation all-star, it takes time and practice. In addition to reflecting on your own performance asking those around you for feedback on what you've done well and where you've struggled is an invaluable part of your path to effective delegation.

EXERCISE: DEVELOP YOUR TEAM BY DELEGATING

After completing this topic, you should be able to recognize how to develop your team through delegation.

In this exercise, you'll identify how to hone your delegation technique in order to develop yourself and your team.

In this exercise, you'll demonstrate that you can

- delegate a task to a person in a way that develops their skills,
- identify how to manage your team's development through delegation, and
- recognize how to develop your delegation technique.

Question

Match each level of trust to an example of delegation action.

Options:

A. Tell

B. Ask

C. Recommend

D. Approve

E. Act

F. Inform

Targets:

1. Give your delegate detailed, step-by-step instructions on what to do

2. Tell your delegate that you'll issue instructions based on their research findings

3. Listen to your delegate's suggestions, then make a decision together

4. Let your delegate decide on the best course of action before you sign off on it

5. Tell your delegate to do whatever seems best, provided there are no negative risks

6. Give your delegate absolute authority and responsibility, asking to be notified of developments

Answer

This action is at the tell level of trust. It's most appropriate for a junior member of your team who doesn't have much experience. It entails telling them exactly what to do.

This action is at the ask level of trust. It involves allowing the delegate to ask about or investigate something, and then telling them what to do once they've returned with their findings.

This action is at the recommend level of trust. It involves getting the delegate to recommend something and then making the decision together based on whatever the delegate suggests.

This action is at the approve level of trust. This is appropriate when dealing with someone who has proven themselves to the extent that you only need to approve and sign off on their decisions.

This action is at the act level of trust. This is the second-highest level of trust. It entails allowing the delegate to act freely within certain limits or boundaries.

This action is at the inform level of trust. It's the ultimate level of freedom and trust, and means your delegate can take whatever decisions he or she deems appropriate. All that you require is that you're informed

of what's happening.

Question

Manuel, a senior engineering consultant, wants to delegate tasks to Josie, a trainee engineer, in a way that will help her develop.

Which actions would contribute toward Josie's development?

Options:

1. Manuel asks Josie to take on some difficult, challenging tasks that he's confident she can handle

2. Having skills that Josie would benefit from learning, Manuel assigns tasks likely to teach those skills

3. Impressed with how Josie handled her most recent task, Manuel assigns a new task that involves greater responsibility

4. While giving Josie interesting and enjoyable tasks, Manuel is careful not to burden her with responsibility, given her inexperience

5. Manuel is careful only to assign tasks that Josie has the skills to perform

Answer

Option 1: This option is correct. In order to develop employees, it's important to delegate tasks that represent a challenge. Challenging tasks are more likely to motivate the delegate, which helps in their development.

Option 2: This option is correct. A delegate develops when you enable and coach the delegate to develop new skills. This sometimes means giving a task to someone even though that person doesn't yet have the skills needed to complete the task.

Option 3: This option is correct. Incrementally increasing a delegate's level of responsibility and showing them more trust each time they prove themselves are important parts of employee development.

Option 4: This option is incorrect. Employees develop when they're

given responsibility, authority, and trust. This should be at a low level at first, increasing incrementally as they continue to prove themselves.

Option 5: This option is incorrect. Part of developing an employee is enabling them to acquire and develop new skills. This can mean assigning tasks from which the delegate will learn new skills.

Question

Overextending and demotivating delegates are the two main risks to avoid when delegating tasks.

Match each risk to examples of ways to avoid it. Each risk matches to more than one example.

Options:

A. Overextending

B. Demotivating

Targets:

1. Ensure that your delegate has all necessary support and assistance

2. Try to match the delegate's level of ability with the level of responsibility involved

3. Avoid delegating a task to someone that they've done hundreds of times before

4. Try to give your delegate the opportunity to try something new and challenging

Answer

This is an example of an action that would avoid overextending a delegate. Assigning a task that carries too much authority or autonomy, without the appropriate support and assistance, can easily go wrong.

This is an example of an action that would avoid the mistake of overextending a delegate. When delegating a task, it's important to ensure there's a balance between the task delegated and the delegate.

This is an example of an action that would avoid demotivating a dele-

gate. It's a mistake to delegate something to someone that is likely to be mundane and boring to them. Doing so would be demotivating.

This is an example of an action that would avoid the mistake of demotivating a delegate. Assigning a task that challenges the delegate brings excitement and motivation.

Question

Timothy, an HR director at an economic consulting firm, is reflecting on his delegation performance.

Which questions should he ask himself as part of his review of his own performance?

Options:

1. Did I adequately prepare the tasks I delegated?

2. Did I make helpful suggestions to assist the delegate?

3. Did I follow up and support the delegate?

4. Did I provide enough instruction on what needed to be done?

5. Did the delegate adequately acknowledge my seniority and authority?

6. Did the delegation experience enhance my managerial abilities?

Answer

Option 1: This option is correct. When reviewing your delegation performance, it's important to consider whether you adequately prepared the delegation. This would include giving consideration to which tasks are being delegated to which individuals.

Option 2: This option is correct. When reviewing your delegation performance, it's important to consider whether you were encouraging. This includes being helpful, offering coaching and guidance, and trying to keep the delegate motivated.

Option 3: This option is correct. When reviewing your delegation performance, it's important to consider whether you offered sufficient supervision. *This includes following up and supporting the delegate.*

Option 4: *This option is correct. When reviewing your delegation performance, it's important to consider whether the delegation was an educational experience for the delegate. This means assessing whether you provided enough instruction and guidance on what was required.*

Option 5: *This option is incorrect. While it's perhaps important and possibly beneficial for a delegate to recognize a delegator's seniority, it isn't a measure that should be assessed when reviewing one's delegation performance.*

Option 6: *This option is incorrect. Enhancing or improving the delegator's managerial skills isn't an objective of delegation, so this wouldn't be something to consider when assessing delegation performance.*

Question

Getting feedback from those around you is an effective way to develop your delegation technique.

Identify the examples of best practices for getting feedback on your delegation style.

Options:

1. Assure your team that you genuinely want to know what they think

2. Emphasize that you're genuine and serious about wanting to get better at delegation

3. Assure your delegates that you value and respect what they have to say

4. Collect all of your delegates' responses and make an overall assessment

5. Consider making it mandatory for team members to provide feedback

6. Ask each team member to comment on one other team member's feedback

Answer

Option 1: *This option is correct. Getting feedback begins with talking to your team and convincing them that you want them to speak openly and candidly.*

Option 2: *This option is correct. It's important to convince your delegates that you truly want to improve your delegation style and that their feedback is an important part of this happening.*

Option 3: *This option is correct. It's important that your delegates genuinely believe that you value, respect, and want to hear their views. Otherwise they may be inclined to hold back or tell you what they think you want to hear.*

Option 4: *This option is correct. Once you've spoken to your delegates, you should collect the*

feedback together, focusing in particular on feedback directly related to your delegation style. When you have this information, you're better positioned to make an overall judgement on how you performed.

Option 5: *This option is incorrect. When soliciting feedback, there needs to be an atmosphere of trust and openness. Forcing delegates to provide feedback wouldn't be helpful in this regard.*

Option 6: *This option is incorrect. This is not an example of a best practice for getting feedback. It could be viewed as a breach of trust and privacy, which could inhibit people from being open and honest.*